Flags

By Julie Haydon

W0099618

A lot of countries
have flags.

This is the flag of Australia.

It is red and white and blue.

It has six stars.

This is the flag of New Zealand.

It is red and white and blue.

It has four stars.

This is the flag of China.

It is red and yellow.

It has five stars.

This is the flag of Malaysia.

It is red and white

and blue and yellow.

It has a star and a moon on it.

This is the flag of Canada.

It is red and white.

It has a leaf on it.

This is the flag of America.

It is red and white and blue.

It has stars and stripes on it.

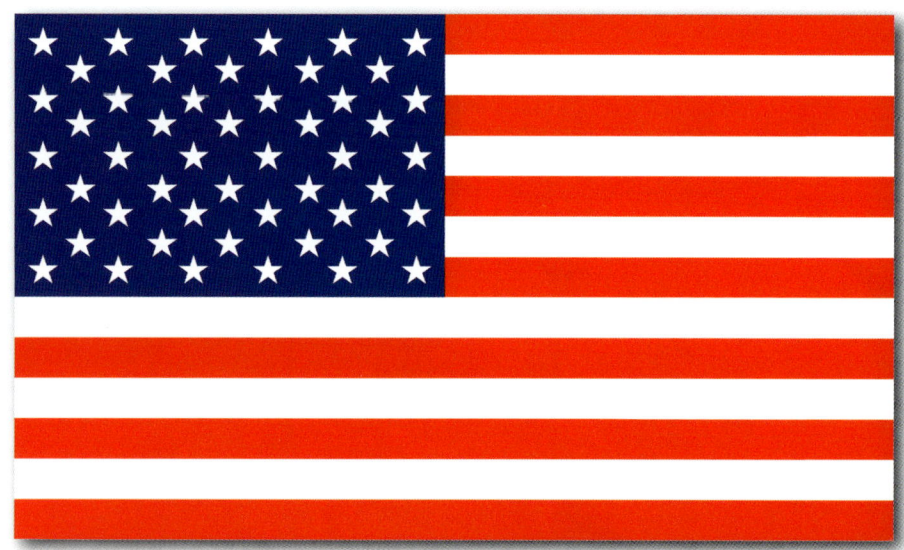

It is fun to wave the flag
of your country.